Singing for Inanna

poems in English and Arabic
by Jenny Lewis and Adnan Al-Sayegh

translations by Ruba Abughaida with the poets

❧

introduction by Daniel Ferguson

❧

CD of recorded poems with oud music by Patricia de Mayo and Tarik Beshir, played by Patricia de Mayo;
also featuring incidental music by Naseer Shamma and 'Anthem for Gilgamesh' by Jenny Lewis

MULFRAN PRESS

First published 2014 by Mulfran Press
2 Aber Street, Cardiff CF11 7AG, UK
www.mulfran.co.uk

The right of Adnan Al-Sayegh, Jenny Lewis and Daniel Ferguson
to be identified as authors of this work has been asserted in accordance with the Copyright, Designs and Patents Act, 1988.

Poems and translations © the poets and the translators

All translations are by Ruba Abughaida, Adnan Al-Sayegh and Jenny Lewis, except 'Song for Innana
/ Ishtar' which was translated by Taj Kandoura and edited by Adnan Al-Sayegh.

Introduction © Daniel Ferguson

song 'Anthem For Gilgamesh' © Jenny Lewis
recorded at Truck Studios, Oxfordshire
published by Spinney Records, March 2014

CD production by Rowland Prytherch

Front cover image © Suad Al-Attar, used by kind permission of the artist.
"He sang to her ... until words slept" (oil on canvas | 1991 | 27x36 inches)

ISBN 978-1-907327-22-3

Supported using public funding by

ARTS COUNCIL
ENGLAND

LOTTERY FUNDED

Printed by imprint**digital** in Devon [info@imprintdigital.net]

Adnan Al-Sayegh was born in al-Kufa, Iraq, near the Euphrates River. He has published eleven collections of poetry, including the book-length *Uruk's Anthem* (Beirut 1996) and won several international awards. He left his homeland in 1993 and since 2004 he has been living in exile in London.

Jenny Lewis is a poet, playwright and songwriter. Her recent work includes *After Gilgamesh* (Mulfran Press, 2011) a verse drama for Pegasus Theatre, Oxford and *Taking Mesopotamia* (Oxford Poets/ Carcanet, 2014). She teaches poetry at Oxford University.

Ruba Abughaida is a Palestinian-Lebanese poet, short-story writer, novelist and translator who lives and works in London. Her short story 'The Scirocco Winds' won the 2014 Writers and Artists Historical Fiction Prize.

Suad Al-Attar is a renowned Iraqi painter whose work is in private and public collections worldwide. Her many awards include first prize at the International Biennale in Cairo in 1984. She has lived in London since 1976.

Naseer Shamma is an Iraqi oud player and composer who began studying the oud at the age of 12. He writes and plays oud music for CDs, theatre, films and television and is revered and loved worldwide.

Patricia de Mayo was born in Munich, Germany. She is a singer, composer and multi-instrumentalist. She studied piano at the Guildhall School of Music and holds a Masters in Arabic Music from SOAS, University of London.

Rowland Prytherch is a freelance recording engineer and music producer based in north London. A graduate of the SAE institute in Recording Arts, he is also a multi-instrumentalist musician who has performed at major festivals and toured the UK and Europe.

Chris O'Donnell is widely experienced in the field of broadcast media production, working for the BBC. He produced the 'Anthem For Gilgamesh – Jenny Lewis and Adnan Al-Sayegh' video for the Arts Council funded 'Writing Mespotamia' project, which is now posted on YouTube.

Acknowledgements

We should like to thank John Prebble and Arts Council South East for their generous support of this project. We should also like to thank Daniel Ferguson and Irving Finkel at the British Museum for making possible the 'Writing Mesopotamia' programme and the workshop participants for their creativity and warm fellowship.

Leona Medlin, of Mulfran Press, has been a most kind, patient, generous and inspired editor and superb enabler of our work and kept us going through thick and thin. This book and CD would not exist without her. We thank her from our hearts for her belief in us and for helping us build bridges between worlds with our poetry. We should also like to thank Suad Al-Attar for allowing us to use her beautiful painting '"He sang to her…until words slept" for our cover; Ruba Abughaida for her accomplished translations of our work, Taj Kandoura for his translation of 'Song to Inanna/ Ishtar' into Arabic; Mouthanna Al-Sayegh for his careful setting of the Arabic texts throughout the book and on its cover and to all Adnan's family for their dedication and helpfulness towards this project.

We give thanks and respect to the great Naseer Shamma for allowing us to use his incomparable music on the CD. We warmly thank our friends Patricia de Mayo and Tarik Beshir for their inspirational oud compositions and Patricia, especially, for working so closely and hard with us to create and play most of the music that accompanies our poetry.

Finally, our thanks go to Rowland Prytherch for his extraordinary creative and technical skill in arranging and producing 'Anthem for Gilgamesh' and for all the friends and artists who helped to bring this song into being – especially Chris O'Donnell who created the film which can be seen on YouTube and stands as a testament to the goodwill of everyone involved in this project towards the people of Iraq. We hope your suffering will soon be at an end and that you will be able to resume safe, peaceful and productive lives again in the very near future.

'Anthem for Gilgamesh' - www.youtube.com/watch?v=y0rLG80jQko

NOTE: I should also like to acknowledge my debt to Andrew George for the inspiration his translation of the *Epic of Gilgamesh* (Penguin Classics, 2003) has provided for my own re-visioning, and to thank Stephen Knight and Blake Morrison at Goldsmiths College, London University, for their support and encouragement of my endeavours.

Jenny Lewis
Oxford, August 2014

Writing Mesopotamia, British Museum, April 2014

Jenny Lewis approached myself and Irving Finkel (Assistant Keeper Ancient Mesopotamian) at the Museum back in July 2013 with the proposal for the project that would become the 'Writing Mesopotamia' workshops and performance held in April 2014.

In the British Museum's adult programmes team we are always looking for new and creative ways to help our audiences engage with the ancient art in our collection. Jenny's proposal was immediately appealing in that it exhibited a profound connection with the ancient Mesopotamian material on display in our galleries through Jenny's practice, previous works and her personal story, but also represented a unique opportunity for those with little previous experience of this culture to become inspired by it and share their creative journey.

The three creative writing workshops focussed on the history and culture, legends and art and the major literary accomplishments of Ancient Mesopotamia. Participants were invited to explore the works in the galleries and consider them as starting points for a creative response through poetry. From considering basic questions such as 'what material is a given object made from?' to the imaginative gaps opened up by considering who may have made the pieces and what emotions they hoped to evoke, through to deeply personal reflections on the images and memories that the objects may recall, we hoped that the participants would interpret this inspiring material in ways only they could.

Participants' ideas were then brought back to the classroom where Jenny and the inspirational Iraqi poet Adnan al-Sayegh helped them structure and shape their thoughts. The resulting works were quite remarkable and I must thank Jenny for suggesting from the outset that participants should have the chance to showcase their work at a concluding performance at the Museum two weeks following the final workshop.

Reading your original and often personal works to a large public audience might be thought to be 'daunting' before 'exciting', and given that participants did not necessarily have any prior experience of writing creatively, this could easily have been an opportunity that many felt was beyond them. I think it's credit to the trust that Jenny and Adnan built throughout the project that a third of the participants signed up to perform at the event in the Stevenson Lecture Theatre on 27th April.

The readings on that afternoon were very special and they served to re-emphasise the many creative responses that the Writing Mesopotamia programme provoked. More than that, it was a great way to celebrate the culture of Mesopotamia represented by the British Museum which was also reflected by the moving readings of poems in this book by Jenny and Adnan, accompanied by a beautiful oud performance by Patricia de Mayo and singing by Divine Chipanga and Abigail Hawkesworth. Everyone who arrived at the Museum that day came as individual performers, but left as a community who valued this remarkable ancient culture all the more for having shared their perspectives and made new friends in the process of doing so.

In this publication you have the opportunity to read and hear Adnan and Jenny's own work from the time of the Writing Mesopotamia project and I'm very grateful that this collection can act as a legacy for the small community that I'm proud to say this project brought together.

Daniel Ferguson
Head of Adult Programmes
British Museum, April 2014

A video of the 'Writing Mesopotamia' workshops readings at the British Museum March/ April 2014 is online at http://vimeo.com/102782344

A video of Jenny Lewis and Adnan Al-Sayegh reading in the second half of that event is at http://vimeo.com/95647489

Song For Inanna/Ishtar

Your eyes, the twin rivers
Tigris and Euphrates,
two great flocks winding through the night
mirrored by star-fields.

Capriciously, you dispose of your lovers –
the gardener, the water-carrier, the leopard-headed king.
You indulged him a full year until he was led
uncomplaining to the edge of the furrow.

Your breath smells of hooves and spit.
Your body emits the shimmer of bulls.
The grain of your groin is horned and cloven.
When you open your legs
your vastness swallows us whole.

Jenny Lewis

أغنية إلى اينانا / عشتار

عيناكِ؛ النهران التوأمان
دجلةُ والفراتُ
هما سربان عظيمان، يلتفان خللَ الليلِ
يعكسان حقلاً من النجومِ.

بنزوة؛ تركلين عشاقَك:
البستانيُّ، والسَّقَّاءَ، والملكَ الذي له رأسُ فهدٍ،
غَمَستهِ بالملذاتِ، لعام كامل، حتى تمَّ اقتيّادُهُ
إلى حافةِ اللحدِ، دونَ أنَّ يشكّو.

لأنفاسكِ رائحةُ حوافرَ وبصاقٍ
جسدُكِ ينفثُ وميضَ الثيرانِ
وملتقى فخذيكِ مصدرٌ للطاقةِ والإغواء
وعندما تفتحين ساقيكِ
فإن اتساعَكِ يزدردُنا جميعاً.

جني لويس

Second Song To Inanna/Ishtar

How did you materialise from the cuneiform board
fixed to the wall in the museum?

You looked in surprise and confusion
at the faces of the tourists and students surrounding you –

while you were chanting psalms of love,
with modesty and music that are yours alone

they were cautiously touching
(aware of the cameras and the eyes of the guards)
your firm breasts.

How has lapis-lazuli come
out of hard stone?
Oh Inanna/ Oh Ishtar/ Oh Aphrodite/ Oh Venus
Oh genie of my poem!

Who brought you here, Oh stranger like me?!
Who brought you, Oh stranger?!

Trains, histories, armies, and kisses have marched by.
Trees, wars and exiles have marched by.
Al Sayyab and Edith Sitwell have marched by –

while we stand on Embankment bridge listening to the murmurings of the
Tigris and the Thames –
two parallel histories that can neither meet nor part
and so leave us regretting what each has lost by the other's absence.

"Oh generous Tigris!"
"Sweet Thames, run softly,
till I end my song…"

…the sound of jazz from a homeless girl rises from under the bridge
and we dance along with the night to her music

أغنيةٌ ثانيةٌ إلى اينانا / عشتار

كيفَ طلعتِ
من لوح مسماريٍّ،
في حائطِ
المتحفِ

التفتِ بذُعرٍ وحَيرةٍ
إلى وجوهِ السّياحِ والطلابِ، مشدودةً إليكِ..
كانوا – وأنتِ ترتّلين مزاميرَ الحبِّ، بخَفَرٍ وموسيقى لا يليقان إلّا بكِ -
يتلمّسون بحذرٍ (خشيةَ عيون الكّاميرات والحارس)
نهدَكِ النافرَ

كيف قد طلعَ اللازوردْ
من الحجرِ الصلدْ
يا اينانا / يا عشتار / يا افروديت / يا فينوس
يا..
جنّيةُ القصيدة

- مَنْ أتى بكِ، إلى هنا؛ يتها الغريبةُ مثلي!؟
- مَنْ أتى بكَ، أيهذا الغريبُ!؟

مرّتِ القطارات والتواريخُ والعساكرُ والقُبل
مرّتِ الحروبُ والأشجارُ والمنافي
مرَّ السيّابُ وإديث سِتْويل Edith Sitwell
ونحنُ - على جسر إمباكمنت Embankment - نتأملُ خريرَ دجلة والتايمز،
كأنهما مسارُ تاريخين؛ لا يلتقيان ولا يفترقان
ونتحسّرُ على كلِّ ما ابتلعهُ الغيابُ منا

"يا دجلة الخيرِ... يا.."
".. أيها التايمز العذبُ، تسلسلْ بهدوءٍ
ريثما أُكمِلُ أغنيتي"

يصّاعدُ جازٌ من عازفةٍ متسوّلةٍ، في نفقِ الجسرِ
فنرقصُ والليل على موسيقاها،

until orange blossom flowers between our fingers
and the columns of the bridge, the roads, the shops, the pages grow green
as far as Walt Whitman.

When we surface we find our boat is rudderless –
not even Uta-napishtim can steer a drunken boat…
Oh Inanna, how do we get back to Uruk, destroyed by the flood?

We are washed from depths to depths,
passing river bank after river bank.

We didn't know that exile would go on so long,
that our journey would only bring loss.

So come close, let poetry be our country,
poetry, love, the flute and wine… how beautiful these countries are,
how creative, how expansive.

At the end of the night
you go back to your board, in the museum,
while I go back to my papers;
to play, to bleed –
and between us is a poem.

حتى يورقَ بين أصابعنا القدّاحُ
وتعشبُ أعمدةُ الجسرِ، الطرقاتُ، الحاناتُ، الصَفَحاتُ...
وصولاً حتى والت وايتمن Walt Whitman

طَفَونا، لا الدَفَّةُ تدري أين؟
ولا أوتنابشتم، والمركبُ ســـــــــــــكرانْ
يا إينانا.. كيف نعودُ لأوروكَ، وقد دمّرها الطُّــــــــوفانْ

تتهادى فينا اللُجَّةُ تِلْوَ اللُجَّةِ،
شُــــــــــطآنٌ تطوي شطآن

ما كنا نَحسبُ أن المنفى سيطولُ،
ورحلتُنا لمْ تَجنِ غيرَ الخُســـــــــــــران

فتعالي؛ يكن الشعرُ لنا وطناً،
والحبُّ، النأيُّ، الكأسُ... وما أجملها من أوطانْ
بل ما أبدعها، ما أوسعها من أوطانْ.

آخرةَ الليلِ...
تعودين إلَى لوحِك، في المتحف
وأعودُ إلى أوراقي؛ أعزِفُ، أنزِف
وبيننا القصيدة!

Adnan Al-Sayegh
May 2013

عدنان الصائغ
مايو ٢٠١٣

The Wise Man Uta-Napishtim Advises Gilgamesh

'You're wearing yourself out with all this stress.'

The Epic of Gilgamesh, Tablet X

Gilgamesh, you're headed for an early grave,
you're riddled with discontent
yet your life could end at any moment –
cut off like a reed in the reed bed.

The gorgeous young man, the lovely girl –
in a flash, death could hack them down:
yet we go on grabbing as much as we can, feathering
our own nests, squabbling over money, starting wars:

        while all the time, the river
rises and floods, the mayfly skims the water,
the sun blazes down on us each day, until all of a sudden –
        it's over!

Jenny Lewis

الرجلُ الحكيمُ، أوتونابشتم؛ ينصحُ گلگامش

"لقد ألبستَ نفسَك كلَّ هذا الجهدِ".
- ملحمة جلجامش، اللوح الخامس -

يا گلگامش، أنكَ تتجهُ لقبرِك مبكراً،
أنتَ مدجّجٌ بالسخطِ
حتى أن حياتَكَ قد تنتهي في أيةِ لحظةٍ -
مقطوعةً كقَصَبةٍ في سريرِ القَصَبِ

الشابُ البهيُّ، الصبيةُ المحبّبةُ -
قد يقطعُهُما الموتُ في ومضةٍ، إرْباً إرْباً:
لكننا نستمرُ - ما استطعنا - في انتزاع ريش
أعشاشِنا، متنازعين على النقودِ، بادئين حروباً:

بينما طَوَال الوقتِ،
يطفو النهرُ ويفيضُ، ذبابةُ مايو تنزلقُ فوق الماءِ،
الشمسُ تتوهجُ فينا كلَّ يومٍ، وفجأةً -
ينتهي كلُّ شيءٍ!

جني لويس

Siduri The Tavern Keeper Advises Gilgamesh

'I can look you in the eye, Tavern Keeper,
but I can't face death.'

The Epic of Gilgamesh, Sippar Tablet

Gilgamesh, what's wrong with you?
You'll never find what you're looking for:
when the gods gave humans life
they also gave them death.
They kept eternity for themselves.

For this is human destiny.

But you, Gilgamesh, eat! Drink!
Enjoy yourself! Put on your best clothes,
wash your hair, have a relaxing bath!
Make the most of what's precious to you –
your child's hand in yours,
the arms of your loving wife.

For this too is human destiny.

Jenny Lewis

سيدوري؛ صاحبةُ الحانةِ، تنصحُ گلگامش

"أستطيعُ النظرَ في عينيكِ، يا صاحبة الحانة،
لكنني لا أستطيعُ مواجهةَ الموتِ".
- ملحمة جلجامش، لوح سيبار -

ما خطبكَ؟ يا گلگامش
إنك لن تجدَ ابداً ما تبحثُ عنه:
عندما منحتِ الآلهةُ الحياةَ للبشر
منحتهم الموتَ أيضاً.
واحتفظوا لأنفسهم بالخلود.

وهذا هو مصيرُ البشر.

لكنك، يا گلگامش؛ كُلْ! اشربْ!
متعْ نفسَكَ! ارتد أحسنَ ثيابِكَ،
اغسلْ شعرك، خذْ حماماً للاسترخاء!
استفدْ للأقصى مما هو نفيسٌ لك -
يدُ ابنكَ في يدكَ،
حضنُ زوجتِكَ المحبةِ.

وهذا هو مصيرُ البشرِ أيضاً.

جني لويس

Ninsun's Prayer To The Sun God Shamash

Gilgames, don't rely on your strength alone.'
The Epic of Gilgamesh, Tablet III

A wild cow in the wilderness is a moving oasis
A wild cow brings her shadow
A wild cow brings comfort

Lady Wild Cow Ninsun fought Gilgamesh's fervour
Flinging her fearful words at Shamash
"Why! Why have you made my son so restless?"

SEVEN TIMES she went into the inner sanctum
Seven times crossed the sacred threshold
Seven times she smoothed herself with tamarisk
          and saponaria

Then she put on a clinging dress
Hung precious pendants round her breasts
Heightened herself with a headdress of gemstones
Until Aya herself was outshone

Ninsun shone like Shamash's own
The Goddess-Queen lit up the first rays of dawn.
Her harlots threw themselves to the ground in awe.

She mounted the spiral stair of the ziggurat
Approached the altar of almighty Shamash
The garden pearled with smoke as her censer swung
And her words twisted up with the sweet-smelling incense

'Shamash –
    when you open the gates of morning for the herds to stream
       out… and barley and wheat awake in the earth
Shamash –
    when your touch glistens the fur of wild animals… and princes
    of the sky and underworld bow down to you
        Keep your burning eye on Gilgamesh and Enkidu

ابتهالُ نينسون لإلهِ الشمسِ؛ شماش

"يا گلگامش؛ لا تثقْ، بقوتكَ وحدها"
- اللوح الثالث من ملحمة گلگامش -

بقرةٌ بريةٌ؛ في البراري، كما واحةٌ متحركة
بقرةٌ بريةٌ تجيءُ بظلالها
بقرةٌ بريةٌ تجلبُ الراحةَ

السيدةُ، البقرةُ البريةُ، نينسون؛ صارعتْ شراسةَ گلگامش
تقذفُ بكلماتها المرعبة على شماش
"لماذا! لماذا صيّرتَ ولدي هائجاً أبداً؟"

سبع مراتٍ ذهبتْ إلى المعتكف
سبع مراتٍ عبرتْ العتبةَ المقدسةَ
سبع مراتٍ صقلتْ نفسَها بالأثْل
وأزهارِ الصابونية

ثم؛ ارتدتْ فستاناً لاصقاً
وعلّقتِ النفيسَ حولَ نهديها
مزدهيةً بإكليلٍ من الأحجارِ الكريمةِ
حتى أنها فاقتْ بريقَ أيا

بريقُ نينسون مثلَ نَسْلِ شماش
الإلهةُ - الملكةُ أشعلتْ أشعاعاتِ الفجر الأولى
ومومساتها رمين أنفسهَنّ إلى الأرضِ بهلعٍ

امتطتِ السُلّمَ اللولبيَّ للزقورة
اقتربتْ من مزارِ إله الشمس
وتلألأتِ الحديقةُ بالدخان كأنّ مبخرتَها تتأرجحُ
وتتلوى كلماتُها مع البخورِ ذات الرائحةِ الحلوةِ

"شماش -
حينما تفتحُ بواباتِ الصباح؛ ليتقاطرَ القطيعُ، إلى الخارج...
وليستيقظَ الشعيرُ والقمحُ، في الارض
شماش -
حين لمستكَ تلمّعُ فروَ الحيواناتِ البريةِ... وأمراءُ السماءِ، والجحيم،
ينحنون أمامك
ابقِ عينَك المتقدةَ على گلگامش وانكيدو

On the way to the cedar forest make the long road short
On the way to the cedar forest make the short day long
On the way to the cedar forest
           Keep your burning eye on Gilgamesh and Enkidu

Make the moon guard them at night.
Summon the stars to stand as sentries
           and at first light

Let Aya remind you to harness the winds
         the South Wind, North Wind, East Wind, West Wind,
The blasts, counterblasts, the hurricanes and typhoons, the scorching-winds,
Freezing-winds, gales and tornados

Let them batter abhorrent Humbaba!
Let them SHATTER him, batten him, bruise his face black!
Then let my son finish him off with an axe!

Through your sacred fire
Through myrrh's embers
Grant my desire! [Hear me!]
Grant my desire! [Hear me!]
Oh Shamash – grant my desire. [Hear me!]'

                                 Jenny Lewis

في الدرب إلى غابةِ الأرْز اجعلِ الطريقَ الطويلَ قصيراً
في الدرب إلى غابةِ الأرْز اجعلِ اليومَ القصيرَ طويلاً
في الدرب إلى غابةِ الأرْز
ابقِ عينَكَ المتقدةً على گلگامش وانكيدو

اجعلِ القمرَ يحرسهم اثناءَ الليل
استدعِ النجوم لتصطفَ كما الحُرّاس
وعند أولِ ضوءٍ

دعْ أيا تذكرَكَ لتسخيرِ الرياح:
الريح الجنوبية، الريح الشمالية، الريح الشرقية، الريح الغربية
الانفجارات، الانفجارات المضادة، الأعاصير، إعصار التّيْفُوْن، الرياح-الشّائِطة،
الرياح-المتجمدة، العواصف، والزوابع

دعهم يُبْلون بالضرب خمبابا الكريهَ
دعهم يسحقونه، يُسَمّنونه، يَكدُمون وجهه بالسواد!
بعد ذلك دعْ ولدي يجهزُ عليه بفأسٍ!

بقوة نارِكَ المقدسةِ
بقوةِ جمراتِ شجرةِ المُرّ
هبْ لي رغبتي [اصغِ إليَّ!]
هبْ لي رغبتي [اصغِ إليَّ!]
يا شمّاش - هبْ لي رغبتي [اصغِ إليَّ!]

                  جني لويس

Inanna's Desire For Gilgamesh

'Come Gilgamesh, you shall be my bridegroom.'

The Epic of Gilgamesh, Tablet VI

He was built like a door, solid as cedar,
Thighs like a bull's, brazen and bulging,
He washed his hair so it rippled like the Tigris,
Shook it down his back so it shone like the Euphrates.
Crowned with gold he was glorious and godly.
Gilgamesh was glorious and godly.

As if she'd been hit by lightning
As if a fire was running under her skin
As if she'd forgotten how to …
As if her body was ….

     swung against
     the insides
     of a rung bell
       deafened
     dumbfounded
     in a flash

          Inanna fell.

She shook with desire like a reed in the reed bed.
Inanna, war-goddess, thunderbolt-thrower,
Capable of carnage, savage eradicator,
Opened to Gilgamesh like a small flower…
Her lungs lost their power, her voice became lower
         She sang to him softly, beckoning him over

توقُ اينانا لگلگامش

"يا گلگامش؛ تعالَ، ستكون عريسي"،
- ملحمة گلگامش. اللوح السادس -

كان مبنياً مثل باب، صلباً كالأرْز،
فخذان؛ كما للثورِ، بارزان ومنتفخان
غسلَ شعرهُ فتموّجَ كدجلة،
رماهُ خلف ظهره وأشرقَ كالفرات.
كان بهياً وإلهياً، وقد تُوّجَ بالذهبِ.
كان گلگامش، بهياً وإلهياً.

كما لو أنها قد صُعقتْ ببرق
كما لو أنّ ناراً كانتْ تجري تّحت جلدِها
كما لو كانتْ قد نَسيتْ كيف…
كما لو أنّ جسدَها كان…

متأرجحاً عكسَ
الدواخل
لرنينِ الجرس:
بصممٍ
بخَرَسٍ
بومضةٍ

وقعتْ اينانا.

لقد ارتجفتْ بشهوة كقصبة في سريرِ القصبِ.
اينانا إلهةُ الحربِ، القاذفةُ للِّصاعقةِ،
القادرةُ على المذبحةِ، المستأصلةُ وحشيتَهم،
تفتحتْ لگلگامش كوردةٍ صغيرةٍ…
رئتاها فقدتا قوتهما، صوتها أصبَح خافتاً
غنّتْ له برقٍ، وأوْمَأتْه أن يأتي:

'Come now into my sweet-smelling chamber
In a golden chariot studded with amber,
Drawn by a team of lions and mules,
With bridles of silver and drapes of blue lapis.
As you cross my threshold my door will caress you,
You'll conquer my court as you conquer my heart....

'Our reign will bring bounty, be fertile and fecund,
Each goat shall have triplets, each ewe shall have twins:
Our donkeys and horses shall outrace the wind,
Our ox every day shall plough a deep furrow,
Our orchards and farmland shall give a full harvest,
Our seas with a rich crop of silver be blessed.

Only come to me, Gilgamesh,' Inanna said,
'And lie close to me on my perfumed bed.'

Jenny Lewis

تعال الآنَ إلى مخدعي ذي الرائحة الطيبة
في عربة ذهبية مرصعةٍ بأحجار الكَهرمان،
مجرورةٍ بثُلّةٍ مَن أسودٍ وبغالٍ،
مع ألجِمَّة فُضيّةٍ وستائرَ من لازوردٍ أزرق.
وأنتَ تعبُرُ عتبتي، بابي، سيضمانك،
ستحتل حَرَمي كما استعمرتَ قلبي...

عهدُنا سيجلبُ سخاءً،وسيكون مثمراً وخصباً،
كلّ عنزةٍ ستحظى بثلاثة توائم كلُّ شاةٍ ستحظى بتّوَم،
حميرُنا وخيولُنا ستسابقُ الريحَ،
ثورُنا سوف يحرثُ كلَّ يوم أخاديدَ عميقةً،
بساتينُنا وأرضُنا الزراعيةُ سوف تعطي محصولاً وفيراً،
بحارُنا الغنيةُ بِغلّتِها من الفضّةِ ستكون مباركةً.

تعالَ إليّ فقط، يا گلگامش"، قالتْ ايننا،
"واضطجعْ بقربي على سريري العطرِ".

جني لويس

Gilgamesh's Grief For Enkidu

When may the dead see the rays of the sun?

The Epic of Gilgamesh, Tablet IX.

Gilgamesh's grief was like a ravenous eagle
eating him night and day. Wandering in the wilds,
he cried for his friend Enkidu and also for himself.

He was like a speared lion in the wilderness, hugging his grief for Enkidu to
his chest; filled with rough thoughts, wretched and sorrowful, far from home
his grief burst its fetters, the heavy wounds of his heart hurled hurt onto the
hard ground.

A hero must never speak of grief but Gilgamesh was crying out.
He was filled with pain, not just for Enkidu but for himself,
having to follow his friend into the harrowing half-light of the Underworld,
live in half-light like an owl, covered in feathers, like an owl and never again
see the light of the sun.

Dust to dust, ashes to ashes, Gilgamesh was looking for Uta-napishtim,
the Flood survivor, to ask for the gift of eternal life. He couldn't bear to go
into the Underworld and never again see the light of the sun.

He woke abruptly in the moonlight.
There was the Moon God, Sin, like a great lamp in the sky,
and all around him, lions, waiting to take his life from him.

Gilgamesh wielded his axe, once, twice.
The felled lions gave up their lives to the King of Uruk.
Gilgamesh ate their flesh, dressed himself in their skins.

Afterwards, he grew gaunt, he wandered woeful in the wilderness
dressed in lion skins, sleeping little, waiting always for sunrise,
to feast his eyes on light.

He asked the Sun God Shamash:
How much light is there left and where is darkness hiding?
Can the dead ever see the sun again?

حزنُ گلگامش على انكيدو

"متى يمكنُ للميتِ أن يرى أشعةَ الشمس؟"

- اللوح التاسع، من ملحمة گلگامش -

حزنُ گلگامش كان كنسرٍ متهاوٍ
يتآكلُهُ ليلَ نهارَ. هائماً فِّ البراري،
وقد بكى لرفيقه انكيدو، ولنفسه أيضاً.

كان مثل أسد مطعون في البراري، ضاماً لصدرِه حزنَهُ لانكيدو
ممتلئاً بأفكارٍ مضطربةٍ، بائساً وحزيناً،
بعيداً عن وطنه. كُرْبَتُهُ فجَّرَتْ أغلالَها،
وجروحُ قلبِه العميقةُ ألقتِ الألمَ على الأرض الصلبة.

لا يصحُّ لبطلٍ أَنْ يتحدثَ عن حزنٍ، لكن گلگامش كان يصرخُ.
كان محتشداً بالألم؛ ليس لانكيدو و فقط، بلْ لنفسه،
حاجتُهُ لتتبّع رفيقِه في ضوءٍ باهتٍ مروِّعٍ، من العالَم السفليِّ،
وهو يعيشُ في ضوءٍ باهتٍ، مثل بومةٍ؛ مغطّى بريشٍ، مثل بومةٍ؛ ولن يرى ثانيةً،
ضوءَ الشمسِ.

من غبار إلى غبار، من رمادٍ إلى رماد، وگلگامش كان يبحثُ عن اوتانبشتم،
الناجي مِّن الطوفان، ليطلبَ هبةَ الحياةِ الأبدية. لم يكن ليتحمّلَ أن يذهبَ
إلى العالَم السفليِّ، وأَن لا يرى ضوءَ الشمسِ ثانيةً.

استيقظَ فجأةً على ضوء القمر.
كان هناك إلهُ القمر سين، مثل مصباح عظيم في السماءِ،
وكلَّ ما حوله، ليوثٌ، بانتظارِ انتزاع حياته منّه.

گلگامش هوى بفأسِه؛ مرةً، وأخرى.
الليوثُ المتهاوية منحوا حياتَهم لملك أوروك.
گلگامش أكلَ لحومَهمْ، ألبسَ نفسَهُ جلودَهم.
فيما بعدُ، أصبحَ نحيلاً وهامَ حزيناً في البراري
مرتدياً جلودَ أسود، قليلَ النومِ، منتظراً بزوغ الشمس، دائماً،
لتستمتعَ عيناهُ بالضوء.

سألَ انكيدو إلهَ الشمس شماش:
كم بقي هناك من ضوءٍ، وأين تختبئُ العتمةُ؟
وهل يمكن للموتى أن يروا الشمسَ ثانيةً؟

Shamash replied:
Gilgamesh, what are you looking for? You can't live forever in the light.
When the gods made humans, they kept eternity for themselves.

***

Gilgamesh reached the twin mountains of Mashu
which stretch from the underworld up into the highest reaches
of the sky. The gates were guarded by scorpion-beings
who protect the rising sun with mountain shadow.

When Gilgamesh saw them he reeled back, recoiling.
The scorpion-man recognised his godliness, but the scorpion-woman
also detected his human-ness:

He is two thirds god and one third human she said.
And they questioned Gilgamesh about his long travels
which he later set down on a tablet of stone.

Jenny Lewis

أجاب شماش:
يا گلگامش عما تبحثُ؟ إنك لن تعيشَ تحت الضوء الى الأبدِ
عندما خلقتِ الآلهةُ البشرَ، احتفظوا بالأبدية لأنفسِهمْ.

* * *

وصلَ گلگامش إلى الجبلين التوأم لـ ماشو
اللذين يمتدان من العالم السفليِّ إلى أعلى مدىّ
في السماءِ. البَواباتُ كانتْ محروسةٌ بالكائناتِ الحيّةِ
اللاتي يحمين الشمسَ الطالعةَ بظلِّ الجبلِ.

عندما رآهم گلگامشُ قفزَ راجعاً، بنفور
العَقربُ - الذكرُ أدركَ ألوهيتَهُ، لكنْ العَّقربَ - الأنثى
أدركتْ انسانيتَهُ أيضاً:

قالتْ: ثلثاهُ إلهٌ وثلثُ بشرٍّ.
واستفسروا مِن گلگامش عن سفراتِهِ الطويلةِ
التي دوّنها أخيراً على لوحٍ من الحجرِ.

جني لويس

I Need You

Like the earth, parched, prays for rain to pour from the clouds
Like the clouds, streaming with radiance, need the vastness of the sky
Like the sky, heavy with stars, needs to be lifted up by the Lord God
Like the Lord God, in order to forgive us, needs our faults
Like my faults only exist because I'm a dreamer, a bewildered and unaware poet
Like poetry and wine are from you, in you, about you and for you
    (Beautiful, flowering, with kohl-darkened eyes)

I need you

To explain life's meaning and my reason for being,
Your beauty confirms and is endless, I have reached you …
    (And I cannot reach…)

أريدكِ..

وكما الأرضُ؛ مُقْفِرَةٌ، تتضرّعُ للغيم أن يهطلا ..
وكما الغيمُ؛ يحتاجُ حقلَ السماواتِ، يركضُ والهيولى جَذلا
كما والسماواتُ؛ مثقلةٌ بالنجوم، وتحتاجُ ربّاً لِيرفعَها للعُلا
وكما الربُّ؛ يحتاجُ أخطاءَنا، ليضربَ في وسع غُفْرَانه مَثَلا
وكما خطأي لا يكون؛ إذا لَمْ أكنْ شاعراً حالِماً حائراً غَمِلا
وكما الشعرُ والخمرُ؛ منكِ وفيكِ وعنكِ إليكِ:
بهاءً ووورداً ومكتحلا

أريدكِ...

كيما أؤكّدُ معنى الحياة، ومعناي؛
كيما يُؤكّدُ حُسنُكِ لامنتهاهُ، وصلتُ إليكِ..
ولنْ أصِلا....

                                        Adnan Al-Sayegh
                                        May 2013

عدنان الصائغ
مايو ٢٠١٣

Extracts from *Uruk's Anthem*

Uruk's Anthem is one of the longest poems ever written in Arabic literature (549 pages) and gives voice to the profound despair of the Iraqi experience. It has been described as beautiful, powerful and courageous – and at the same time nightmarish and terrifying. It took twelve years to write (1984-1996). Eight years of that time saw the Iran-Iraq War in which Adnan was forced to fight. He suffered greatly, seeing many of his friends killed and spending eighteen months in an army detention centre, a disued stable and dynamite store, that was dangerously near the border with Iran.

Parts of *Uruk's Anthem* were adapted for the stage and first performed in 1989 and then in 1993, at the Rasheed Theatre in Baghdad where the play received wide acclaim but also angered the government. For this reason Adnan was forced to flee the country with his family and seek asylum first in Amman then in Beirut and then Sweden, where extracts of the play were translated into Swedish, with the help of the Nobel Laureate, Tomas Transtromer who became a lifelong friend. Since 2004, Adnan and his family have been living in exile in London.

The extracts of *Uruk's Anthem* in *Singing for Inanna* are published for the first time in English – a first step towards a fuller translation of this important and historic text.

§

Uruk is the city of Gilgamesh and symbol of the god Dumuzi and the temple of the goddess Inanna. It is a Sumerian city that preserved its name all through the Arab Islamic era known as "Warka". It is mentioned in the Torah as Uruk and in Greek and Roman as Urki. Its remains today can be found approximately 220 km south of eastern Baghdad and at a distance of approximately 20 km east from the Euphrates. A shore of the Nile that used to be part of the Euphrates runs through it. Its remains appear in the form of a circle and they were uncovered by a German delegation in 1913, 1928 and 1953 as part of a study conducted on the valley of the Euphrates.

§

مقتطفات من نشيد أوروك

"نشيد أوروك"؛ واحدة من أطول القصائد فيما كُتب في الأدب العربي (549 صفحة) وهي تكشفُ عن عمق اليأس في التجربة العراقية. وقد وُصفتْ بأنها "جميلة وقوية وشجاعة وهي في الوقت نفسه مرعبة مثل كابوس". استغرقتْ كتابتها اثني عشر عاماً (1984-1996) من ضمنها ثماني سنوات من الحرب العراقية الايرانية كان فيها الشاعر ضمن الخدمة العسكرية الإلزامية. عانى الكثير خلالها، ورأى عدداً من أصدقائه يُقتلون في تلك الحرب. كما قضى عاماً ونصفاً مُعاقباً جندياً في اسطبل مهجور للحيوانات، وهو مكان خطر لاستخدامه أيضاً كمخزنٍ لصناديق العتاد، ولقربه من الحدود مع ايران.

مقاطع من قصيدة "نشيد أوروك" كانت قد أُعدتْ للمسرح، حيث قُدم جزؤها الأول عام 1989، وبعدها قُدم جزؤها الثاني عام 1993، على مسرح الرشيد ببغداد، حيث نالت المسرحية اشادة واسعة، لكنها بالمقابل أغضبت السلطات الحكومية. لهذا السبب اضطر الشاعر إلى مغادرة وطنه مع عائلته. ولجأ إلى عمّان، وبعدها إلى بيروت، ثم السويد. وهناك أُعدت من القصيدة نفسها أيضاً مسرحية بالاشتراك مع قصائد الشاعر السويدي توماس ترانسترومر (الحائز على جائزة نوبل)، وقد ربطتهما صداقة مستمرة. منذ عام 2004، والصائغ وعائلته يعيشون في منفاهم في لندن.

هذه المقتطفات من "نشيد أوروك" تُترجم إلى اللغة الإنجليزية وتُطبع لأول مرة في هذا الكتاب "غناءٌ لـ اينانا".. انها خطوة أولى نحو ترجمة كاملة لهذا النص المهم والتاريخي.

أوروك؛ مدينة كلكامش، ورمز الإله دموزي، ومعبد الإلهة إينانا. وهي المدينة السومرية التي حافظتْ على أسمها في العهد العربي الإسلامي بهيئة الوركاء "الورقاء" وورد ذكرها في التوراة بصيغة أرك وفي المصادر اليونانية والرومانية باسم أورخي وتقع بقاياها الآن على نحو 220 كم جنوب شرق بغداد وعلى مسافة نحو 20 كم شرق مجرى الفرات الحالي ويمر فيها شط النيل المندرس الذي كان مجرى الفرات القديم وهي مسورة على هيئة شبه دائرة وقد أظهرت التنقيبات الأثرية الحديثة التي أجرتها البعثة الألمانية عام 1913 و 1928 و 1953 نتائج مهمة في معرفة أطوار حضارة وادي الرافدين.

(1)

We dumped the bags, empty as truth,
on a hard street by Naybur's minarets and followed
                              the carts
                    that were munching our history as if it was hay

Enough of the flute will make you drunk on my tears
Enough wine and bread, and I will sing for you…

at the gates of Nanmakh's temple
Marduk the sorcerer blows on his quill
and parts the sky
in my name and yours:
              attached
                    – to the skyline –
                              is the arch of Lazord
where Juno rages, ordering her scattered guards
                    to grab the wind by the scruff of its neck

(2)

Tireseus laughs: Love cannot be buried
yet Juno buries it
out in the wasteland, leaving it half-covered,
              its penis exposed
to the starving dogs

Some thieves swiped letters
from the wall
              to lead them to
                              treasure
but they found only an old rat
              that flicked his tail in the direction of the hoard
as he gnawed the flood epic

We ran to help stem the flood
but the guard at the Museum of Babylon stopped us with –
Visits are prohibited

---

(١)

تركنا الحقائبَ فارغةً كالحقائقِ
فوق رصيفٍ مدائنِ نيبور كي نلحقَ
القاطراتِ
التي مضغتْ تبنَ تأريخنا،

يكفي قليلٌ من الناي كي تسكري بدموعي
ويكفي قليلٌ من الخمرِ والخبزِ كيما أغني..

على سورٍ معبدِ ننماخ
ينفخُ ساحرُ مردوخ ريشتَهُ
فيشقُّ الفضاءَ
بأسمي وأسمِكِ
ملتصقين
- على لوحةِ الأفق -
قوساً مَن اللازورد
فتغضبُ جونو وتأمرُ حراسها المترامين
أن يمسكوا عنقَ الريحِ

(٢)

يضحكُ منها تايريسياس: لا حبَّ يُدفنُ
تدفنهُ
في العراءِ إلى النصف،
تاركةً عضــوَهُ
للكلابِ المجيعةِ

لكنَّ بعضَ اللصوصِ أزالوا الحروفَ
عن السورِ،
كي يستدلّوا
على الكنزِ
لم يجدوا غيرَ فأرٍ عجوزٍ
طوى ذيلَهُ باتجاهِ الخِزانةِ
يقرضُ ملحمةَ الطوفان

ركضنا إلى الثقبِ كي نوقفَ الفيضان
فأوقفنا حارسُ المتحفِ البابليِّ:
- الزيارةُ ممنوعةٌ ..

(3)

....
....

I want
    an autumn
       to ripen
          this
            whimper
    into an anthem to Uruk
        that is the sum
          of the earth

....
....

Every time they pick up his books
    and throw them
       at the toilet door
he dips his feet into ink
      and blood
and hurries over the lines
to write
the history of Uruk

....
....

(4)

I see lightning flicker
       under Ishtar's eyelids.
but in the sea, I only catch sight of
what a stranger returns to his family:
        a corpse

---

(٣)

....
....

أريدُ
خريفاً
لأنضجَ
هذا
النشيجَ،
نشيداً لأوروك
يختصرُ
الأرضَ

....
....

كلما جمعوا كتبَهُ
ورموها
ببابِ المراحيضِ
يغمسُ أقدامَهُ بالمحابرِ
والدم
ثم يهرولُ فوق السطورِ،
ليكتبَ
تأريخَ أوروك

....
....

(٤)

أرى في البروقِ الغبوقَ الذي يترقرقُ
في جفنِ عشتار.
لكنني لا أرى في البحارِ سوى
ما يردُّ الغريبَ إلى أهلهِ:
جثةً

or stamped boxes
lost in the torrent
..............his reward is to return
for them to wake up to the shadow of an icon
                  and a girl made of straw
who only knows love at the kitchen door
....
....

(5)

      and I open my eyes to the sea

The ECG machine was faulty, the curtains drawn, the surgeons gathered
round my body
           with scalpels
I shouted: *Let me tell you what I saw*
but they wouldn't listen
and the professor began cutting me – over a morgue of text – busy with his
students
          so I closed my eyes and slept deeply

I saw the planets kneeling to me
and the resurrection, ablaze with lightning, crammed with naked crowds
overflowing with their mistakes...

and Israfil blew his horn:
Wake up you sleeping people from your crippled centuries!

I shouted: *Where is God?*

Dust settled on their faces when they woke, terrified, in their pyjamas...
and God stretched himself and flicked through my thick book.
So this is this my life?

Running in hell screaming:
Where are the sins of the tyrants?
The bartender grabbed me:
              Quiet!

أو صناديقَ مختومةً
هائماً في العباب
.... غنيمته بالإياب
ليصحو على ظلِّ ايقونةٍ
وفتاةٍ من القشِ
لا تتقنُ الحبَّ إلا بباب المطابخ
....
....

(٥)

أفتح عيني على البحرِ

كان جهازُ اي. سي. جي عاطلاً، والستائرُ مسدلةً، والاطباءُ منكفئين
على جثتي
بالمشارط
صحتُ: اتركوني أقصُ لكم ما رأيتُ..
فلم يمنحوني انتباهاً
وراحَ الخبيرُ يفصّلني - فوق مشرحةِ النصِ -
منشغلاً بتلاميذه
فأسدلتُ جفني ونمتُ عميقاً..

رأيتُ الكواكبَ تسجدُ لي
والقيامةَ ذات البروق تضجُ بحشدِ العرايا
تفوجُ بسيلِ الخطايا..

واسرافيل ينفخُ في بوقه:
انهضوا يا نيامَ القرونِ الكسيحةِ...

صحتُ: أين الإلهُ؟

فهبَّ الغبارُ يغطي الوجوهَ التي نهضتْ في بجاماتها فزعاً..
وتمطى الإلهُ يقلّبُ دفتري الضخمَ...
تلك حياتي إذن؟

راكضاً في الجحيم أولولُ:
أين ذنوبُ الطغاة؟
فامسكني نادلُ البارِ:
صَهْ

(6)

We would have gone on building these lands
    as God wanted in his Babylonian dream –
      water and prayers rippling over the steps of its hanging gardens

but they destroyed us,
built a prison from our dried blood
and called it a homeland
then said: *be grateful for your country*
....

No sea for us to cover in boats
Oh you that sleep on the stones of the impossible revolution,
      no sand or saliva:
I saw my blood in the stamps stuck on by deportees.....
Why are you wandering by yourself
Life is – the land that you seek.....
....
....

(7)

These ever flowing torrents, where do they go?
Where do these tears go?
The dust of our ancestors is still under our feet so how do their boots step on it –
how do they step on it
      without the ground crying out?

I shout: *this country is ours*
how can we clean it from under our nails?
Each part of its trees used to pulse from our blood to the veins of the leafy branches,
      flowering.......

This dust is raised, driven by centuries of civilisation
    This fog lies heavy on our chests on the way to God's hall.
Our mistakes shine in the crystals
and the rustle of distant winds is the sound of our ancestors
coming from hard stone

(٦)

وكنا سنبقى نعمّرُ هذي البلادَ
كما شاءها الربُّ في حلمه البابليّ
جناناً معلقةً، يترقرق فوق مدارجها الماءُ والصلواتُ

ولكنهم هدمونا
أشادوا على دمنا المتيبّس، زنزانةً
وادعوا أنها وطنٌ
ثم قالوا: هنيئاً بما يخصبُ البلدُ
....

لا بحرَ نثلمهُ بالمراكبِ
يا أيها النائمون على حجرِ الثورةِ المستحيلة
لا رمل أو زبدٌ
رأيتُ دمي في الطوابعِ يلصقها المبعدونَ..
إلى أين تسعى بنفسكَ؟
إن الحياةَ - البلادَ التي تبتغي.........
....
....

(٧)

هذي السيولُ التي لا تكفُّ عن الجريانِ إلى أين تذهبُ؟
هذي الدموعُ إلى أين؟
هذا الترابُ الذي تحتنا من رفاتِ الجدودِ
فكيفَ تدوسُ عليه بساطيرهمْ
دون أن تصرخَ الأرضُ

أصرخُ هذا المدى أرضنا
كيف ننزعها من أظافرنا
كلُّ نسغٍ بأشجارها كان ينبضُ من دمنا في عروقِ الغصونِ الوريقةِ
يزهرُ....

هذا الغبارُ مثارُ سنابكنا في أديمِ الحضارةِ
هذا الضبابُ تحشرج أنفاسنا في الممرِ إلى صالةِ اللهِ
لامعةٌ بالكريستال أخطاؤنا..
وحفيفُ الرياح البعيدةِ أصواتُ أسلافنا
قادمون من الحجرِ الصلدِ..

(8)

Is this Euphrates
nothing but our rippling blood from the age of Sumer?
.........flowing into the pockets of governments
that flay us with salt and revolutions?
We come and go like waves in the mouth of the sea, dirtied...
nothing is created on our shores except for the dead

All things dissipate
And we are nothing but horses on a race to eternity
So why were we born with a rope round our necks
Swinging in the wind, in this exile.....
                                in this land?

(9)

I am raised by the anthem
            to the heart of Uruk
I throw shadows in a country that has no shadows except for the legacy left by
an armoury of stains and statues

Seasons come and fade away
armies come and fade away
kings come and stay....
one of them builds a castle from our skulls while another and another
destroys them
            to build a pigeon's nest
and each has a poet and a poet and a poet and a poet
and a historian and a historian and a historian......

....
....

(٨)

هل كانَ هذا الفراتُ
سوى دمنا المترقرقِ من عهدِ سومر
..... حتى مصبِّ الحكوماتِ
تكشطُ عن جلدنا المِلحَ والانقلاباتِ..
نأتي ومضي كما موجةٌ في فمِ البحرِ يزفرها...
لا نخلّفُ فوق السواحلِ غيرَ الزبَدْ

كلُّ شيءٍ بدْ
وما نحنُ إلّا خيولُ سباقِ الأبدْ
فلماذا ولدنا، وفي عنقِنا حبلٌ مشنقةٍ
تؤرجحنا الريحُ ذاتَ المنافي.....
وذاتَ البلدْ

(٩)

صاعداً في النشيدِ
إلى قلبِ أوروك،
ألقي الظلالَ على وطنٍ لا ظلالَ لهُ غير ما خلّفتهُ البنادقُ
من بقعٍ وتماثيل

تأتي الفصولُ وتذبلُ
تأتي الجيوشُ وترحلُ
تأتي الملوكُ وتبقى..
يشيّدُ أحدهم قلعةً من جماجمنا
ليهدمها آخررررررر
ليشيّدَ برجَ حمامٍ
وكلُّ له شاعر ررررررررر
ومؤرخ خ خ خ خ خ خ....

....
....

Anthem For Gilgamesh
(song performed on the accompanying CD)

First I thought you were a mirage
but you soon made me your city –
Gilgamesh by Uruk's wall
wound a strand of wool round Inanna's heart...

We walked in the rain by the Euphrates
heard Eve singing in her garden
she was clothed in innocence
naming the birds.

Oh Gilgamesh, come home!
Your people need you like the rain.
Oh Gilgamesh, come home –
I need your DNA beside me again.

The genie said *I am on my way to paradise*
to look for my father
and you held out your hand –
offered to show her the way.

My Gilgamesh, stay safe in Uruk
inside the citadel I've built you a sky,
look up from your pain and bewilderment
you'll see the light goes on and on...

Oh Gilgamesh, come home!
Your people need you like the rain.
Oh Gilgamesh, come home –
I need your DNA beside me again.

'When we surface we find our boat is rudderless –
not even Uta-napishtim can steer a drunken boat...
Oh Inanna, how do we get back to Uruk, destroyed by the flood?

We are washed from depths to depths,
passing river bank after river bank.

We didn't know that exile would go on so long,
that our journey would only bring loss'

We walked in the rain by the Isis
heard Eve singing in her garden
she was dressed in flowers
spreading the word.

The genie said *I'm on my way to paradise* ... (repeat)

Oh Gilgamesh, come home!
Your people need you like the rain.
Oh Gilgamesh, come home –
I need your DNA beside me again.

We walked in the rain by the Tigris
heard Eve singing in her garden
she was made of miracles
healing the world.

My Gilgamesh, stay safe in Uruk.... (repeat)

Jenny Lewis

Lines spoken in Arabic after the first repeat of the chorus are from
'Second Song to Inanna / Ishtar' and given here in the English translation

A video 'Anthem For Gilgamesh – Jenny Lewis and
Adnan Al-Sayegh' is available to watch on YouTube.

Singing For Inanna — the CD

Track 1: The Moon Fades by Naseer Shamma (extract) *5.08 minutes*

Track 2: Song for Inanna/Ishtar by Jenny Lewis (English & Arabic) *3.16 minutes*

Track 3: Second Song to Inanna/ Ishtar by Adnan Al-Sayegh (Arabic & English) *9.17 minutes*

Track 4: Uta-napishtim's advice to Gilgamesh by Jenny Lewis (English & Arabic) *2.06 minutes*

Track 5: Ninsun's prayer to the sun god Shamash by Jenny Lewis (English) *5.29 minutes*

Track 6: Ninsun's prayer to the sun god Shamash by Jenny Lewis (Arabic) *5.41 minutes*

Track 7: Siduri's advice to Gilgamesh by Jenny Lewis (English & Arabic) *2.13 minutes*

Track 8: I need you by Adnan Al-Sayegh (Arabic & English) *4.37 minutes*

Track 9: Inanna's desire for Gilgamesh by Jenny Lewis (English) *3.24 minutes*

Track 10: Inanna's desire for Gilgamesh by Jenny Lewis (Arabic) *4.49 minutes*

Track 11: Tender Breeze by Naseer Shamma (extract) *3.43 minutes*

Track 12: *Uruk's Anthem* extract, parts 1-9 by Adnan Al-Sayegh (Arabic & English) *24.28 minutes*

Track 13: Anthem for Gilgamesh *5.07 minutes*
Lyrics and music by Jenny Lewis with a poem extract from 'Second Song to Inanna / Ishtar' written and spoken by Adnan Al-Sayegh. Music arranged and produced by Rowland Prytherch, performed and with additional composition by Joe Bennett (strings), Tarik Beshir (oud), Jon Berry (guitar), Ed Hawkesworth (drums), Alison Bentley (piano, harmonies), Rowland Prytherch (mandolin). Sung by Jenny Lewis with Tom Hawkesworth, Gail Ferguson, Manda Joyce, Isobel Harris and Divine Chipanga (chorus) and Abigail Tarisai Hawkesworth (soloist). Recorded at Truck Studios, Oxfordshire, November 2013.

Bonus: hear 'Gilgamesh's grief for Enkidu' by Jenny Lewis in English and Arabic on the Mulfran Press *Singing for Inanna* web page.

All poems written and spoken by Jenny Lewis and Adnan Al-Sayegh, translated by Ruba Abughaida with the poets (except for 'Song to Inanna / Ishtar', translated by Taj Kandoura and Adnan Al-Sayegh).

Music accompanying poems composed and played by Patricia de Mayo with additional theme on 'Second Song to Inanna / Ishtar' by Tarik Beshir.

All poems and translations first published by Mulfran Press 2013, 2014 except 'Siduri's Advice to Gilgamesh' and 'Uta-napishtim's Advice to Gilgamesh', English versions first published in *Taking Mesopotamia* (Oxford Poets/ Carcanet 2014).

Featuring incidental music by Naseer Shamma.

'Anthem for Gilgamesh' lyrics and music by Jenny Lewis, published by Spinney Records 2014

Supported using public funding by

LOTTERY FUNDED | ARTS COUNCIL ENGLAND